T0083145

Embertides

Suite for Organ

HILARY TANN

Commissioned by the American Guild of Organists
for the 2014 Biennial National Convention
in Boston, Mass.

MUSIC DEPARTMENT

OXFORD
UNIVERSITY PRESS

OXFORD
UNIVERSITY PRESS

Great Clarendon Street, Oxford OX2 6DP,
United Kingdom

Oxford University Press is a department of the University of Oxford.
It furthers the University's aim of excellence in research, scholarship,
and education by publishing worldwide. Oxford is a registered trade mark
of Oxford University Press in the UK and in certain other countries

© Oxford University Press 2013

Hilary Tann has asserted her right under the Copyright, Designs
and Patents Act, 1988, to be identified as Composer of this Work

First published 2014

Impression: 1

All rights reserved. No part of this publication may be reproduced,
stored in a retrieval system, or transmitted, in any form or by any means,
without the prior permission in writing of Oxford University Press

Permission to perform the works in this anthology in public
(except in the course of divine worship) should normally be obtained
from a local performing right licensing organization, unless the owner or
the occupier of the premises being used already holds a licence
from such an organization. Likewise, permission to make and exploit a
recording of these works should be obtained from a local mechanical
copyright licensing organization

Enquiries concerning reproduction outside the scope of the above should
be directed to the Music Rights Department, Oxford University Press,
at music.permissions.uk@oup.com or at the address above

ISBN 978-0-19-339901-3

Music origination by Jon Bunker

Printed in Great Britain on acid-free paper by
Caligraving Ltd, Thetford, Norfolk

Contents

1. Advent (Winter) 1

2. Lenten (Spring) 4

3. Whit (Summer) 10

4. Michaelmas (Autumn) 14

Composer's note

Embertides consists of four separate movements that take their inspiration from the roughly equal divisions of the church year—Advent, Lent, Whitsun, and Michaelmas. These divisions in turn pay homage to earlier, secular traditions—Winter (seeding), Spring (awakening), Summer (harvesting), and Autumn (vintage). The cycle is unified by references to verses from the 11th-century plainsong sequence 'Veni Sancte Spiritus'; in addition, each piece contains hints of hymns appropriate to each season. The work may be performed as a concert suite or individual movements may be used separately within church services.

The composer is grateful to Alfred V. Fedak (Albany, NY) for his professional assistance in selecting appropriate organ registrations.

Duration: 15 mins (Advent: 3′20″, Lenten 3′40″, Whit 3′40″, Michaelmas 4′00″)

Embertides was first performed by Heinrich Christensen at the National Convention of the American Guild of Organists, June 25 and 26, 2014, at the First Church in Boston, MA.

1. Advent (Winter)

HILARY TANN

© Oxford University Press 2013

Printed in Great Britain

OXFORD UNIVERSITY PRESS, MUSIC DEPARTMENT, GREAT CLARENDON STREET, OXFORD OX2 6DP

The Moral Rights of the composer have been asserted. Photocopying this copyright material is ILLEGAL.

22
27
32
rit.
Meno mosso ♩ = 60
37
p
Opt. Solo
(Sw.)

41
rit.
pp
Fl. 4'
46
Andante ♩ = 69
Sw.
Ob. 8'
p
50
Più mosso ♩ = 80
allarg. molto
Fl. 8',
Str. 8'
molto
57
Andante ♩ = 69
Meno mosso ♩ = 60
16', 8'

2. Lenten (Spring)

Sw.: Fl. 8', 2'
Ch.: 8', 2⅔'
Ped.: 16', 8'

HILARY TANN

© Oxford University Press 2013

13
Ch.
17
f
Sw.
21
Ch.
24
Sw.

28
Ch.
Sw.
mp
31
p cresc.
Add
34
Add
37
cresc. sempre

40
rit.
f
Meno mosso ♩. = 42
43
47
Leggiero ♩. = 56
Sw.
Fl. 8', 2'
p
51

54
Ch.
mp
58
Sw.
cresc.
61
Add
rit.
Meno mosso ♩. = 42
64
f

68
rit.
Leggiero ♩. = 56
73
p
Sw.
Fl. 8', 2'
77
80
allarg.

3. Whit (Summer)

Sw.: Fl. 8', 4', 8' str. cel., 4' couplers
Ped.: Fl. 4', Pr. 2'

HILARY TANN

© Oxford University Press 2013

a tempo
Più vivo ♩ = 80
15
f
p
Sw. Pr. chorus
and mixture
21
accel.
27
Vivo ♩ = 92
f
33
mf
p
8'
p

39
rit.
44
p Original registration
Molto flessibile ♩ = 72
50
p
Chant-like
Fl. 4', Pr. 2'
mp
54
p
mp

58
p
Più vivo ♩ = 80
62
f
67
16', 8'
72
rit. al fine
pp

4. Michaelmas (Autumn)

Gt.: Pr. 8', Fl. 4'
Sw.: Pr. 8', 4', mixture
Ped.: 16', 8'

HILARY TANN

© Oxford University Press 2013

20
Gt.
Sw. f
Gt. mf
25
Add
31
dim.
rit.
Meno mosso ♩= 76
rit.
37
Cornet p

Danza ♩ = 92
41
Sw. p
cresc.
46
51
Gt. mf
55
Sw. f

59
Gt. mf
63
dim.
Sw.
Gt.
67
Sw.
Gt. mp
rit.
Meno mosso ♩ = 76
rit.
72
Cornet p

76
a tempo (♩ = 76)
Sw. p
espress.
81
rit.
Più lento ♩ = 63
rit.
Gt. mf
espress.
86
Danza ♩ = 92
Sw. p
cresc.
91
cresc. sempre

96
f
101
Gt.
rit.
106
Meno mosso ♩ = 76
rit.
111
ff